CREATIVE CONFLICT

IDEA-RICH LEADERSHIP STRATEGIES FOR TEAM SUCCESS

BOB 'IDEA MAN' HOOEY
AUTHOR, LEGACY OF LEADERSHIP

3rd edition – updated 2018

Box 10, Egremont, Alberta, Canada T0A0Z0
www.SuccessPublications.ca

Welcome to our new leaders' edge success series.

Many of these min-books will be uploaded primarily as Kindle Shorts to assist you in enhancing your leadership and honing your skills to lead your teams to a higher level of productivity.

They are designed to be short reads with solid content that you can apply quickly.

Enjoy!

Bob 'Idea Man' Hooey
www.ideaman.net
www.BobHooey.training
www.SuccessPublications.ca

A word as we start

"There are countless ways of attaining greatness, but any road to reaching one's maximum potential must be built on a bedrock of respect for the individual, a commitment to excellence and a rejection of mediocrity."
Buck Rogers (Former CEO of IBM)

Effective leadership is a commitment to interaction and connection with people, some of whom are difficult to deal with on occasion.

One thing I have learned in my many years, in a variety of leadership and team roles, is conflict naturally happens when people come together.

Conflict results when people with varying viewpoints, cultures, experiences and agendas attempt to connect or co-operate in a relationship, a venture or even a common cause of *great* importance.

CONFLICT is simply a bi-product of the interaction and connection between people. Handling it effectively is a part of the leadership process!

Conflict left *'unresolved,'* can tear organizations and teams apart. It can destroy friendships and relationships built over long periods of time.

Conflict has some '*positive*' benefits too!

However, to gain these positive benefits one needs to deal effectively with the conflict. It takes work to find resolution that promotes and proceeds growth and productive change. I'll cover some of these *'benefits'* in this mini-book.

This is where the '*effective*' leader steps into the picture.

Keeping their eye on the **big picture** and the reason for coming together helps the leader maintain their perspective and a more objective viewpoint.

Seeing *everyone* as a potential champion and a value-added part of helping the team and its various members succeed.

I've pulled excerpts from my **'Coaching for Optimal Results – Bringing out the best in people!'** workbook and have expanded by including additional thoughts, tips and resources for your leadership library.

In the short time, we have together I'll seek to assist you in framing your role as a leader in relationship to effectively dealing with creative conflict. You will have **the '*gift*' of conflict** this year. How you handle that *'gift'* will determine your growth as a leader. It will also impact your gift of leadership.

Resolve to be an *'effective'* leader and welcome *'creative conflict'* as an opportunity to help your team grow and succeed.

Bob 'Idea Man' Hooey
Author, Legacy of Leadership
www.ideaman.net
www.BobHooey.training
www.SuccessPublications.ca

Table of Contents

A word as we start 3
Table of Contents 5
Qualities of an EFFECTIVE Leader 6
Using Team Conflicts 8
So, you have a problem… that's great! 17
A personal note from Bob 23
Creative conflict-based problem solving 24
Copyright and license notes 28
Acknowledgements, credits, and disclaimers 29
Bob's B.E.S.T. publications 31
What they say about Bob 'Idea Man' Hooey 33
About the author 34

Qualities of an EFFECTIVE Leader

Congratulations on tackling a leadership role. It will be challenging, growth enhancing and ultimately helping you make a significant contribution.

Good leaders are in no small part also coaches, champions and cheerleaders for their respective teams – that is, if you want your team to grow and succeed!

Becoming a good leader who is an effective ***coach*** means learning to draw on your abilities and skills to train those who need your help in reaching your common or shared goals.

Here are the traits of successful and effective leaders and coaches. These qualities help immensely when dealing with teams and the potential conflict in their interaction as your progress toward the goal or project laid out as a challenge.

Good Communications Skills
Use clear and concise language to instruct, direct, and coach
Use your active listening skills
Maintain eye contact

Solid understanding of the subject
Comprehensive understanding of the subject or skills
Willingness to draw from your background
Willingness to grow and update your professional development

Experience
It helps if you have done the job personally
Previous experience in training

Patience
New people can make mistakes while they learn
It often takes a few tries to get it right
Remember how it was for you when you started out?

Interest in being a leader, coach and trainer
You need to enjoy helping people
Seeing people grow and learn makes you feel good
Seeing others' success gives you a sense of pride and satisfaction

Genuine respect for other people
People view you as being knowledgeable
People view you as being trustful and trustworthy

Well-developed sense of humor
You see the humor in the situation
You don't take yourself or life too seriously

Having and using these traits and skills won't guarantee your success as a leader, trainer or coach; but they will give you a better chance to do the job effectively. They will also lay the groundwork needed to effectively deal with conflict that arises from your team's interaction.

Enjoy the journey, have fun and keep your eye on the larger picture.

Remember, it is not about you! It's about helping them win! When they win, you win!

Where would you rate yourself in each of these areas?

Using Team Conflicts

"It's important to talk to people in their own language. If you say it well, they'll say, 'Wow, he said exactly what I was thinking.' And when they begin to respect you, they'll follow you to the death."
Lee Iacocca *(former CEO of Chrysler)*

Conflict is too often viewed as something groups should avoid. When we normally think of conflict, we visualize people arguing, fighting, name-calling, and/or stress and tension.

Conflict can start with a simple misunderstanding or lack of clarity in our communication. As leaders, when we take the time to speak their language, we reduce the potential for conflict.

Although conflict can be produced in negative ways, there are many positive benefits **creative conflict** can produce for groups. To earn these *'benefits,'* a group must be ready to face **creative conflict** squarely. Our purpose here is to outline how groups can benefit from **creative conflict** by identifying key conflicts early and avoiding some common pitfalls in discussion.

Benefits of creative conflict

Dealing openly with group conflict has several *'positive'* and healthy benefits for the team and its members:

Improve the group's solution

Conflict can help the group produce *'better answers'* because conflict can force groups to confront possible defects or challenges in a solution. Conflict can help group members analyze the specifics of any group's goals, procedures, and solutions to ensure that the best choice for the group is selected.

An absence of conflict in a group decision-making process might be the result of **'group think.'** This 'group think' pitfall has destroyed the creativity, innovation and progress of more groups, companies and organizations than you could imagine.

By allowing **creative conflict** to enter a group decision-making process, the group is more likely to analyze the potential solutions to help in choosing the best solution for the group's needs.

Productivity

Managing conflict helps reduce the amount of time wasted on solutions that are not as effective and that might have a negative effect on the group's productivity. By avoiding conflict, group members are more likely to become distant or withdraw from the group and begin to slack off -- having a negative effect on group productivity.

The sad thing is this happens under the surface at first and by the time it comes to light it is *almost* too late for the leader to resolve. Keeping conflict and its resolution open and transparent is the secret to keeping people involved and committed. Don't hide it or run from it. As the leader, recognize it, delve deeper into it, or investigate to make sure you know all the details and then deal with it openly and honestly.

Organizational change

Creative conflict helps identify potential problems resulting from procedures, assignments, and responsibilities within groups. By allowing conflict to surface in a group, the group might find that the specific rules and procedures for doing things aren't working or might not be best suited for the group members. Sometimes they are having a detrimental effect on the group.

Allowing for healthy ***creative conflict*** will allow a group the opportunity to change itself to obtain a better, more creatively functioning group.

Awareness

Creative conflict allows individuals to learn more about their own personal conflict style (how they deal with conflict and how they bring it to the table). By identifying and understanding their own conflict style, individuals can learn the strengths and weaknesses associated with their style.

This awareness allows group members the opportunity to learn how their creative conflict style affects others, which helps individuals learn how to anticipate and resolve future conflict situations.

As a leader, this can be invaluable in knowing your own creative conflict style and the styles of those on your teams as well. It will help in finding solutions and coming to a consensus and agreement on resolution.

Personal Development

Creative conflict teaches individuals which conflict styles might be more appropriate in various conflict situations. By dealing with conflict, individuals can begin to learn how to use other conflict styles to produce better resolutions to group conflict. Knowing what works and what hurts can be an invaluable tool for you as a leader. The wisdom is knowing and using them appropriately.

Psychological maturity

Managing creative conflict often helps individuals to become better at learning or exploring how to take the perspectives of others.

By learning how to take the perspective of others, individuals become better at anticipating conflict and concern others might have in the future.

Morale

Addressing creative conflicts allow group members to vent their emotions, release stress, and reduce tensions. By facing conflict together, group members have the potential to become closer to other group members, which can have a positive overall effect on the group's morale.

Detecting conflicts

There are several helpful techniques that allow groups to identify potential conflicts among their members.

These techniques include:

Straw poll

A straw poll is a non-binding vote on a proposal to determine the level of agreement of the individuals within the group. Straw polls have a few drawbacks: it might cause 'group think' to occur, suppress viewpoints that are in the minority, provide a sense of discord, or cause others to feel excluded from the group.

Often, straw polls work best AFTER the group has, at least briefly, discussed concerns of the proposal. When conducting a straw poll, individuals should not be counting who is for or against a specific proposal.

Round robin

A round-robin is designed to allow everyone in the room a moment to speak. In a go-round, ***everyone*** is yielded the floor to discuss the topic at hand.

In a go-round, *each individual* state a position and explains their reasoning behind their position.

Round-robins are very effective for allowing equal time to all individuals in the group. This is especially beneficial for hearing the opinions of quieter group members who often refrain from speaking in an open, unstructured discussion. As a leader, make sure they are engaged and share from their perspective. They might have the secret.

Small Group Discussion

Depending of the size of your group, sometimes it would be beneficial to break the group into smaller group discussions to allow individuals to express their ideas and concerns.

A small group discussion is beneficial when a group is large, pressed for time, and wants to explore the various views of the group. After small group discussion occurs, a member from each group summarizes their discussion to provide the larger group with an understanding of the various positions and ideas within the group. Small group discussions allow for a group to generate various positions available on a topic and help to lead discussions about the various concerns and issues rose by group members.

Fishbowl

After various positions from group members have been identified, a fishbowl can be used to explore the ideas and concerns related to each position. In a fishbowl, representatives for each position are chosen to represent and explain their position and answer any concerns related to this position.

A fishbowl is designed arranged to avoid repetitive arguments from appearing and to expedite the discussion.

A fishbowl is beneficial because it allows all positions to be discussed without having to have everyone in the room overlap their ideas with everyone else.

A fishbowl allows for a condensing the time discussing an issue but does not sacrifice the quality of the discussion.

HP uses something like this as a creative exercise in their corporate culture. They divide their teams into two smaller teams who research a challenge and then come back and advocate their solution. Then a vote is taken on which decision is the better one.

Pitfalls of conflict resolution

Keep in mind that there are some pitfalls in the resolution process and in dealing effectively with conflict in any situation. The road is not always clear and has a few potholes or pitfalls to be aware of when navigating towards a solution or resolution.

Here are some areas (pitfalls) to be kept in mind:

Working on problems that are too general, too large, or not well-defined

Problems that are too general are vague or void in the specifics needed to generate any potential solutions. Working on problems that are too large for the group to handle often results in frustration by the group.

Ill-defined problems are difficult to discuss in any detail. Problems that are either too general, too large, or ill-defined will make discussing the problem and finding solutions difficult and frustrating. Work to break down the problems into manageable, discussion-able pieces.

See **'Why Didn't I THINK of That?'** for some specific suggestions on how to do this. (www.SuccessPublications.ca

for more information on purchasing your own copy for your leadership library.)

Jumping to a solution before really analyzing the problem
Sometimes groups will accept a solution before determining what are the aspects of the specific problem. They often stop at the first *'right'* answer or the first one that fits. This is troublesome because without understanding the entirety of the problem; there is no way to adequately and to accurately assess the suitability, cost, or application of the proposed solution. Often, this pitfall occurs when groups are pressed for time.

Failing to involve critical group members when identifying potential solutions

Although group members do not need to be present when every decision is being made, it is important for the group to determine which group members are essential for dealing with a specific problem.

A general guideline is to make sure that those individuals that are affected by the decision are present when the decision is being made. When this is not done, it will often result in those not involved in the process delaying or resisting buy-in or application. It is time well spent to ensure that those affected are involved in the process. As a leader, this can make or break your long-term success.

Tackling problems that are *'beyond'* the control or influence of the group itself

This pitfall occurs when a group tries to accomplish more than is possible for the group. For example, a student group tried to develop a media campaign to end bicycle related problems on campus. The group decided to develop a series of four-color posters, public service announcements, and several press releases to address this serious concern.

Unfortunately, without the proper funding and contacts within various news organizations such as television stations and newspapers, the student's campaign is not feasible. This can be seen in volunteer organizations, which have operations and members on many levels, and in various locations around the world.

Toastmasters for example operates in over 100 plus countries When members want a change, it must filter its way through the District to the international level where it may not be dealt with unless it is of importance to the organization at large and affects many Districts.

Applying *'pet'* solutions rather than seeking the ideal solution

This often occurs in groups that have people who use competitive styles of conflict management. Often, these '*dominating*' individuals will try to impose their '*pet*' solution and do not allow any other individual within the group to criticize the solution. I have seen that all too often. ☺

The group accepts these 'pet' solutions, in part, as they either wish to either avoid the competitive individual or accommodate the solution. This may be because the conflict does not appear to be one that can be resolved in a collaborative or compromising fashion. Not good in the long run for the health of the group or the growth of the group.

Failing to plan adequately how to implement and evaluate the chosen solution

This pitfall occurs when groups have spent all their energies exploring the various positions and concerns related to the problem. After a long or difficult discussion of positions and concerns, group members become too tired to engage in an active discussion of how to evaluate and implement the solution.

Lots of ideas but no Ideas At Work!

The evaluation of the solution needs to be based on a set of pre-determined criteria developed by the group. In fact, this criterion is better set prior to the discussion of the challenge itself.

Implementation needs to be planned, managed, and monitored. There needs to be resources available and applied to implement the solution.

Without taking the time to properly evaluate and implement the solution, the entire process of developing a solution is virtually useless.

"Man must evolve for all human conflict a method which rejects revenge, aggression and retaliation. The foundation of such a method is love.
Martin Luther King, Jr.

So, you have a problem... that's great!

So, you have a problem, that's great! Are you crazy? Actually...NO! Someone once told me, **"I'd get paid or determine my value, by my ability to solve problems."**

If it was easy, everyone would be doing it, and the competition would be intense. But, as most customers will tell you, most businesses are not in the problem-solving field.

Your ability to solve your client's problems will be directly related to the number of sales and continued growth of your firm. This is what is needed if you want to creatively and profitably enhance your career and move your company and its leadership to the next level.

The more successfully and **creatively you solve these problems**, the more referrals and fans you'll see. The more productive you are personally in being a *solution-oriented* owner, manager, or employee will dramatically affect your paycheck, profits, and career path.

I've developed and applied a **simple 4-stage process for dealing with problems and conflicts**. I've shared this with leaders and their teams around the globe and found it works. This is an effective way to deal **creatively** with customer complaints and concerns as well as other areas of your business and life. These ideas will work with creative and strategic planning, conflict resolution, or in everyday problem solving.

Many of my clients and audiences have a *creative* need to be *productive* in dealing with customers. I've written from that perspective. These steps work in idea generation, brainstorming preparation, and in dealing with company expansion and career enhancement issues just as well. (*This section is excerpted from my* ***"Make ME Feel Special – Idea-rich customer service strategies*** *available from* www.SuccessPublications.ca*)*

Here are the four stages:

Invest time in making sure you fully UNDERSTAND the problem.

The key to understanding is to IDENTIFY the real cause.

Take time to fully explore and DISCUSS all the possible solutions.

Act to SOLVE or fully resolve the problem.

"The Secret to Effective Customer Service" or business development is to systematically and profitably go through this process with your clients.

After the problem/conflict has been successfully resolved, **go the extra mile**. By that I mean, doing something *unexpected* to assist the client or to show them you appreciate the opportunity to prove your commitment to their wellbeing. This will help turn an angry or frustrated client into a fan, or better yet…a champion for you and your business.

Stage One - Understanding the problem/conflict:

Often a problem/conflict is in a perception of a *difference* of what we expected to happen and what *happened*. Here are **three action steps** to help.

Gather ALL the facts. Be thorough and investigate. Let the client talk!

Listen carefully, and don't be defensive. Wait until they've finished talking and ask more questions to draw them out, to find out their REAL concerns. (Why not purchase **'Learn to Listen'** from www.SuccessPublications.ca)

Rephrase or repeat the problem/conflict back to the client to make sure you've heard it correctly and understand what needs to be resolved. Agree on this stage.

It's important at this stage to make sure you don't fall into the trap of denying or trying to avoid the problem/conflict; or worse yet, blaming or attacking someone else, or demonstrating the same negative emotions in response to a customer's complaint.

Just listen and get the facts!

Stage Two - Identify the Real Cause of the Problem:

You might ask yourself or your client a few *probing* questions to find out what may have caused the problem.

What has happened? Listen and ask questions. Get a true assessment of the current situation.

What should have happened? Ask questions and listen carefully. Was perception a problem?

What went wrong? This is where you start partnering with the client.

Keep in mind the true cost of an unhappy client. (*Hint: average cost is 8-16 customers lost for each un-satisfied customer.*)

What future purchases could you expect from this client?

What future business this client could influence?

What the problem at hand costs to rectify?

From research and years of experience, I've noticed that problems/conflicts generally often fall into **four major areas**:

Mechanics or Function - product or service failed to work as expected.

Assembly or use - someone didn't use it correctly or put it together incorrectly.

The People Factor - we make mistakes in how we do something or how we deal with a client.

Client EGO - how this PROBLEM makes them look (good or bad) in their eyes and the eyes of their friends and families.

Stage Three - Explore and DISCUSS possible solutions.

This is possibly the most critical part in the client satisfaction/problem solving process. We need to fully focus and objectively look at the challenge we've partnered with the client to solve.

Here again - a few **simple action steps**.

Suggest options. Take time to explore ALL the options that might effectively help solve this problem or at least minimize the impact.

Ask your customer for their ideas. Very often, they have a solution in mind, or have some good input that will help you mutually resolve it to their satisfaction. If they are a partner in the decision, they will help make it work and will be more inclined to be happier with the results. **Their satisfaction will result in referrals for you!**

Agree on the best solution or course of action. After you've fully explored the options, make sure you both agree on what and when you will do to resolve it. THEN DO IT!

Stage Four - Take ACTION to resolve the problem or conflict.

This is the *completion stage* that builds a foundation for a potential long-term relationship with your *formerly* dissatisfied client. Make this a priority focus for your firm.

Once you've agreed on what needs to be done, move heaven and earth to do it, and do it better and quicker than you've promised.

Remember, they are watching to make sure you were serious about making them happy. This is your chance to prove your commitment.

Again, **three action steps.**

Physically remove the cause of the problem or take steps to retrain if problem was personnel based.

Take corrective action to substitute, replace or repair the product or service.

Ask the client if they are satisfied with the changes and action you've taken.

Going the extra mile. This is where you cement the relationship by doing something extra, something totally unexpected by the client.

Show them you care and are *genuinely* concerned about the *perceived* inconvenience they've experienced. **Apply your creativity to cementing the relationship!**

One note: **Use your complaints as a creative source of product or service development.**

Each one is an opportunity for you to learn how to better serve your clients, refine your service, or improve your product in the market place.

This is also an opportunity to expand your business or service by using these creative solutions as stepping stones, or business building blocks.

Yesterday's problems are today's new and improved products or services.

Want to be a creativity leader? YES! Then learn from each lesson your clients give you. This is an opportunity for you to build a strong foundation for success well into the next decade.

Don't miss the lesson. It might be a "v-e-r-y" valuable one!

"Peace is not the absence of conflict but the presence of creative alternatives for responding to conflict - alternatives to passive or aggressive responses, alternatives to violence."
Dorothy Thompson

A personal note from Bob

I appreciate the privilege to share with you some creative new approaches to problem solving, creative conflict, or strategic planning. I appreciate the opportunity to exercise my creativity and learn together with my audiences and readers. Often, the lessons we discuss, and the ideas generated help me in refining my approach and my program content. At times, they have opened new doors or areas to explore. I would challenge you to use these tips and techniques in your day to day operations, as well as in your personal life. I'm confident you'll find them helpful.

Remember there is always a creative solution!

Share these ideas with your clients and co-workers, so they can take advantage of ways to make their lives more productive and less stressful. Engage the minds of those around you. Often the solution of your problem or creative conflict is hidden in the mind of a colleague, competitor or client.

I realized one of the challenges of speaking within a time frame and having a topic that has so many variables to discuss, was covering the most relevant material. That challenge was one of the reasons I include so much in my learning guides and workbooks.

I've included some of the creative conflict problem-solving models for your future reference and will focus on the ones that might serve you best as you begin to reframe your approach to problems that inevitably appear in your life and career. I hope you enjoy it.

Would you take a moment from time to time to share your success stories with me? (email: bob@ideaman.net) This will serve several purposes. I'd like to know how this material has helped you or your clients. Your successes might just help me add new material or keep this material current and fresh.

Creative conflict-based problem solving

Many problems that a group may face are complex and ambiguous and there are several alternative solutions that might be adopted. That choice can be a challenge in itself.

These types of strategic problems require a more thorough examination of the assumptions and inferences that underlie them and their solutions.

In this kind of situation, team leaders, managers, and strategic planners can use one of two important conflict-based problem-solving techniques: dialectical inquiry and devil's advocacy.

Such conflict-based, problem-solving models stress *'critical evaluation'* over group harmony. This kind of a destructive foundation for future success provides an interesting paradox.

While group morale and interpersonal relations are always at some risk whenever individuals engage in conflict, many problem-solving teams find that structured conflict can yield high-quality results.

Let's briefly describe **two problem-solving models** based on conflict.

Dialectical Inquiry

In the dialectical inquiry approach, the team uses the *'same set of data'* to create or formulate two separate and opposing recommendations and then formally debates these recommendations based on the assumptions that were used to derive them. The philosophy behind this method is that a clearer understanding of the situation and an effective solution result when the assumptions underlying each recommendation are subjected to intense scrutiny and evaluation.

Here is a simple or basic outline of procedures for preparing and carrying out a dialectical debate:

Divide your whole group into two advocate subgroups.

Have one subgroup develop a set of recommendations for solving the problem, making sure to keep a list of all key assumptions and facts that underlie them.

Give a copy of this list and the recommendations to the other subgroup.

After receiving the first group's list of key assumptions, the second group should then set out to develop *'another set'* of plausible counter-recommendations whose assumptions contradict those of the first group.

Once each group has catalogued their key assumptions about the situation and developed their plans for solving the problem, *'structured'* debate between the two subgroups is ready to begin.

Have someone state the problem the group is trying to solve.

Elect an advocate from each of the subgroups to present orally and in writing all key facts, data, and assumptions to the other group. You may have one person do the oral, and a second handle the writing.

After each side has had a chance to make their presentation, the subgroups should then debate both plans, the goal being to expose hidden and/or faulty assumptions in either one.

Once the debate is completed, the *'whole'* group should agree on which assumptions are most plausible and develop and/or fine-tune the recommendations based on these *'surviving'* assumptions.

Devil's Advocacy

Much like dialectical inquiry, the process of using a devil's advocacy for problem solving and decision-making relies on *'structured'* conflict to ensure a high-quality decision is reached.

In this approach, a solid, well-supported argument is laid out for a set of recommendations and then subjected to a grilling evaluation by another person or subgroup.

Those who use devil's advocacy assume that only the best plans will survive such extensive censure.

The following procedures will help you and your team prepare for a round of devil's advocacy:

Divide your team into two subgroups, one of which will serve as devil's advocate.

The subgroup that is not devil's advocate should develop a plan to solve the problem, making sure to write down all key assumptions and facts that support them.

The first subgroup then submits the recommendations and a list of the assumptions that underlie them to the devil's advocacy group.

The devil's advocate group subjects the plan to an intense evaluation, trying to uncover everything that is wrong with their recommendations and inaccurate with the assumptions.

The first subgroup would then go back to their initial plan or recommendation and adjust, edit, or adapt their recommendations based on the *'valid'* criticisms of the devil's advocate group.

"Peace is not absence of conflict, it is the ability to handle conflict by peaceful means." **Ronald Reagan**

Using creative conflict effectively

In both the dialectical approach and the devil's advocacy approach, 'structured' conflict is a central part of fleshing out or defining the soundest recommendations and thoroughly understanding the assumptions that underlie them.

However, there is always some risk involved when individuals engage in creative conflict. For this reason, it is important to develop the right attitude for any creative conflict activity.

Here are some quick tips to help your group use creative conflict-based problem solving effectively:

First and foremost, don't be afraid of creative conflict.

If you don't normally like to engage in creative conflict, remember that this is a structured debate. While you must either give or receive criticism, you don't have to be confrontational and antagonistic to do it.

Remember that critical evaluation is the crux of these creative conflict-based models of problem solving.

Don't mistake legitimate criticism for a personal attack.

Refrain from basing your criticisms on the character of another group member.

In other words, keep your focus on the recommendations themselves, not who made them or why.

Always keep in mind that the goal of subjecting your recommendations and assumptions to an intense critique is to '*develop better ones*' and ensure that the team's plan will ultimately be able to survive the same sorts of critiques from outsiders. **Strive for creative quality.**

Copyright and license notes

Creative Conflict (updated 3rd edition)
Idea-rich leadership strategies for team success

Bob 'Idea Man' Hooey, Accredited Speaker, 2011 Spirit of CAPS recipient. Prolific author of 30 plus business, leadership, and career success publications

© Copyright 2004-2018 Bob 'Idea Man' Hooey

All rights reserved worldwide *No part of this publication may be retained, copied, sold, rented or loaned, transmitted, reproduced, broadcast, performed or distributed in any such medium, or by any means, nor stored in any computer or distributed over any network without permission in writing from the publisher and/or author. Care has been taken to trace ownership of copyright material contained in this volume. Graphics are royalty free or under license. The publisher will gladly receive information that will allow him to rectify any reference or credit line in subsequent editions. Segments of this publication were originally published as articles and/or parts of other books and program materials and are included here by permission of the publishers and authors.* Unattributed quotations are by Bob 'Idea Man' Hooey.

Cover design: **Racheal William**
Photos of Bob: **Dov Friedman**, www.photographybyDov.com
Bonnie-Jean McAllister, www.elantraphotography.com
Frédéric Bélot, www.fredericbelot.fr/fr
Editorial, layout and design: **Irene Gaudet,** Vitrak Creative Services (a division of Creativity Corner Inc.), vitrakcreative.com

ISBN 13: 978-1986879910 ISBN 10: 1986879917

Printed in the United States 10 9 8 7 6 5 4 3 2 1
Success Publications – a division of Creativity Corner Inc.
Box 10, Egremont, AB T0A 0Z0
www.successpublications.ca
Creative office: 1-780-736-0009

Acknowledgements, credits, and disclaimers

As with each of my books, a very special dedication of this piece of myself, to the two people who meant the most to me, my folks **Ron and Marge Hooey**. Sadly, both my parents left this earthly realm in 1999. I still miss our time together and your encouragement and love. I was blessed with the two of you in my life. I've added **George and Lillian Sidor** (Irene's folks) to this gratitude list.

To my inspiring wife and professional proof reader and publications coach, **Irene Gaudet**, who loves, encourages, and supports me in my quest to continue sharing my **Ideas At Work!** across the world. Thank you seems so inadequate for your timely work in helping make my writing and my client service better! I love the time we spend together!

To my colleagues and friends in the National Speakers Association (NSA), the Canadian Association of Professional Speakers (CAPS), and the Global Speakers Federation (GSF) who continually challenge me to strive for success and increased excellence.

To my great audiences, leaders, students, coaching clients, and readers across the globe who share their experiences and enjoyment of my work. Your positive and supportive feedback encourages me to keep working on additional programs and success publications like this updated version. My experience with you creates the foundation for additional real-life experiences I can take from the stage to the page, the classroom to the boardroom.

My thanks to a select few friends for your ongoing support and 'constructive' abuse. You know who you are. ☺

Disclaimer

We have not attempted to cite all the authorities and sources consulted in the preparation of this book. To do so would require much more space than is available. The list would include departments of various governments, libraries, industrial institutions, periodicals, and many individuals. Inspiration was drawn from many sources, including other books by the author; in this updated creation of "Creative Conflict!"

This book is written and designed to provide information on more effective use of your time, as a life and leadership enhancement guide. It is sold with the 'explicit' understanding that the publisher and/or the author are not engaged in rendering legal, accounting, or other Professional services. If legal or other expert assistance is required, the services of a competent Professional in your geographic area should be sought.

It is not the purpose of this book to reprint all the information that is otherwise available. Its primary purpose is to complement, amplify, and supplement other books and reference materials already available. You are encouraged to search out and study all the available material, learn as much as possible, and tailor the information to your individual needs. This will help to enhance your success in being a more effective sales person, leader or professional.

Every effort has been made to make this book as complete and as accurate as possible within the scope of its focus. However, there may be mistakes, both typographical and in content or attribution. Graphics are royalty free or under license. Care has been taken to trace ownership of copyright material contained in this volume. The publisher will gladly receive information that will allow him to rectify any reference or credit line in subsequent editions. This book should be used only as a general guide and not as the ultimate source of information. Furthermore, this book contains information that is current only up to the date of publication.

The purpose of 'Creative Conflict' is to educate and entertain; perhaps to inform and to inspire. It is certainly to challenge its readers to learn and apply its secrets and tips, to challenge them to enhance their skills and leverage their time to create more Productive outcomes. The author and publisher shall have neither liability nor responsibility to any person or entity with respect to any loss or damage caused, or alleged to have been caused, directly or indirectly, by the information contained in this book.

Bob's B.E.S.T. publications

Bob is a prolific author who has been capturing and sharing his wisdom and experience in print and electronic formats for the past fifteen plus years. In addition to the following publications, several of them best sellers, he has written for consumer, corporate, professional associations, trade, and on-line publications. He has been engaged to write and assist on publications by other best-selling writers and successful companies. His publications are listed below.

Bob's **B**usiness **E**nhancement **S**uccess **T**ools

Leadership, business, and career success series

Running TOO Fast (8th edition 2018)
Legacy of Leadership (3rd edition 2016)
Make ME Feel Special! (6th edition 2016)
Why Didn't I 'THINK' of That? (5th edition 2015)
Speaking for Success! (8th edition 2016)
THINK Beyond the First Sale (3rd edition 2017)
Prepare Yourself to WIN! (3rd edition 2018)

Bob's mini-book success series

The Courage to Lead! (4th edition 2017)
Get to YES! (3rd edition 2017)
THINK Before You Ink! (3rd edition 2017)
Running to Win! (2nd edition 2017)
How to Generate More Sales (4th edition 2017)
Unleash your Business Potential (3rd edition 2017)
Learn to Listen (2nd edition 2017)
Creativity Counts! (3rd edition 2016)
Create Your Future! (3rd edition 2017)

Bob's Pocket Wisdom series
Pocket Wisdom for Selling Professionals
Pocket Wisdom for Speakers
Pocket Wisdom for Innovators
Pockct Wisdom for Leaders – Power of One!
Pocket Wisdom for Business Builders

Co-authored books created by Bob
Quantum Success – 3 volume series (2006)
In the Company of Leaders (3rd edition 2014)
Foundational Success (2nd edition 2013)

Bob's Idea-rich leaders edge series
LEAD! *12 idea-rich leadership success strategies*
CREATE! *Idea-rich strategies for enhanced innovation*
TIME! *Idea-rich tips for enhanced performance and productivity*
SERVICE! *Idea-rich strategies for enhanced customer service*
SPEAK! *Idea-rich tips and techniques for great presentations*
CREATIVE CONFLICT! *Idea-rich leadership strategies for team success*

Visit: www.SuccessPublications.ca for more information on Bob's publications and other success resources.

Email: bob@ideaman.net or visit: www.SuccessPublications.ca

Connect with Bob 'Idea Man' Hooey:

Facebook: www.facebook.com/bob.hooey
Success Publications: www.SuccessPublications.ca
Websites: www.ideaman.net www.BobHooey.training
LinkedIn: www.linkedin.com/in/canadianideamanbobhooey
YouTube: www.youtube.com/ideamanbob
Smashwords: www.smashwords.com/profile/view/Hooey
Email: bob@ideaman.net
Creative Office: 780-736-0009
Snail mail: PO Box 10, Egremont, AB T0A0Z0

What they say about Bob 'Idea Man' Hooey

As I travel across North America, and more recently around the globe, sharing my Ideas At Work, I am fortunate to get feedback and comments from my audiences and colleagues. These comments come from people who have been touched, challenged, or simply enjoyed themselves in one of my sessions.

I'd love to come and share some ideas with your organization and teams.

"I still get comments from people about your presentation. Only a few speakers have left an impression that lasts that long. You hit a spot with the tourism people." **Janet Bell**, Yukon Economic Forums

"Thank you, Bob, it is always a pleasure to see a true professional at work. You have made the name 'Speaker' stand out as a truism - someone who encourages people to examine their lives and adjust. The comments indicated you hit people right where it is important - in their hearts. Each of those in your audience took away a new feeling of personal success and encouragement." **Sherry Knight**, Dimension Eleven Human Resources and Communications

"I am pleased to recommend Bob 'Idea Man' Hooey to any organization looking for a charismatic, confident speaker and seminar leader. I have seen Bob in action on several occasions, and he is ALWAYS on! Bob can grab his audience's attention and keep it. Quite simply, if Bob is involved - your program or seminar is guaranteed to succeed." **Maurice Laving**, Coordinator Training and Development, London Drugs

"On very short notice Bob cleared his schedule and graciously presented at our meeting when the original Speaker was unable to attend. **Last week Bob set the tone for our two-day leadership meeting and gave us all a motivational lift.** *His compassion and true interest in people was clear, making him very credible. He shared some great stories, has a wealth of experience and knowledge and it was a pleasure listening to him. His down-to-Earth style makes it easier to retain the information presented. Fantastic job, Bob, and thanks again!"* **Barbara Afra Beler**, MBA, Senior Specialist Commercial Community, Alberta North, **BMO Bank of Montreal**

About the author

Bob 'Idea Man' Hooey is a charismatic, confident leader, corporate trainer, inspiring facilitator, Emcee, prolific author, and award winning motivational keynote speaker on leadership, creativity, success, business innovation, and enhancing team performance.

Using personal stories drawn from rich experience, he challenges his audiences to engage his **Ideas At Work!** – To act on what they hear, with clear, innovative building-blocks and field-proven success techniques to increase their effectiveness.

Bob challenges them to hone specific 'success skills' critical to their personal and professional advancement. Bob outlines real-life, results-based, innovative ideas personally drawn from 29 plus years of rich leadership experience in retail, construction, small business, entrepreneurship, manufacturing, association, consulting, community service, and commercial management.

Bob's conversational, often humorous, professional, and sometimes-provocative style continues to inspire and challenge his audiences across North America. Bob's motivational, innovative, challenging, and practical Ideas At Work! have been successfully applied by thousands of leaders and professionals across the globe.

Bob is a frequent contributor to North American consumer, corporate, association, trade, and on-line publications on leadership, success, employee motivation and training; as well as creativity and innovative problem solving, priority and time management, and effective customer service. He is the inspirational author of 30 plus publications, including several best-selling, print, e-books, and a Pocket Wisdom series. Visit: www.SuccessPublications.ca for more information.

Retired, award winning kitchen designer, Bob Hooey, CKD-Emeritus was one of only 75 Canadian designers to earn this prestigious certification by the National Kitchen and Bath Association.

In December 2000, Bob was given a special CAPS National Presidential award "…for his energetic contribution to the advancement of CAPS and **his living example of the power of one**" in addition to being elected to the CAPS National Board. He has been recognized by the National Speakers Association and other professional groups for his leadership contributions.

Bob is a co-founder and a past President of the CAPS Vancouver & BC Chapter and served as 2012 President of the CAPS Edmonton Chapter.

He is a member of the NSA-Arizona Chapter and an active leader in the National Speakers Association, a charter member of the Canadian Association of Professional Speakers, as well as the Global Speakers Federation (GSF). He retired (December 2013) as a Trustee from the CAPS Foundation. He is currently the CAPS GSF Ambassador.

In 1998, Toastmasters International recognized Bob "…for his professionalism and outstanding achievements in public speaking". That August in Palm Desert, California Bob became the 48th speaker in the world to be awarded this prestigious professional level honor as an Accredited Speaker. In 2018, only 75 people have earned it to date.

He has been inducted into the Toastmasters Hall of Fame on numerous occasions for his leadership contributions. In 2018, he was appointed Region 4 Advisor for Toastmasters International.

Bob has been honoured by the United Nations Association of BC (1993) and received the CANADA 125 award (1992) for his ongoing leadership contributions to the community. In 1998, Bob joined 3 other men to sail a 65-foot gaff rigged schooner from Honolulu, Hawaii to Kobe, Japan, barely surviving a 'baby' typhoon en-route.

In November 2011 Bob was awarded the Spirit of CAPS at their annual convention, becoming the 11th speaker to earn this prestigious CAPS National award. Visit: www.ideaman.net/SoC.htm

Bob pictured here presenting at the AFCP conference in Paris, France

Bob loves traveling, and his speaking and writing have allowed him to visit 54 countries so far. Perhaps your organization would like to bring Bob in to share a few ideas with your leaders and teams around the globe.
Contact him at: www.ideaman.net
Visit: www.HaveMouthWillTravel.com for more information.

"I have been so excited working with Bob Hooey, as he has given inspiration and motivation to our leadership team members. Both at the Brick Warehouse – Alberta and here at Art Van Furniture – Michigan; with his years of experience in working with business executives and his humorous and delightful packaging of his material, he makes learning with Bob a real joy. But most importantly, anyone who encounters his material is the better for it."
Kim Yost, CEO Art Van Furniture, former CEO The Brick

Motivate your teams, your employees, and your leaders to 'productively' grow and 'profitably' succeed!

Protect your conference investment - leverage your training dollars.

Enhance your professional career and sell more products and services.

Equip and motivate your leaders and their teams to grow and succeed, 'even' in tough times!

Leverage your time to enhance your skills, equip your teams, and better serve your clients.

Leverage your leadership and investment of time to leave a significant legacy!

Call today to engage best-selling author, award winning, inspirational leadership keynote speaker, leaders' success coach, and employee development trainer, **Bob 'Idea Man' Hooey** and his innovative, audience based, results-focused, **Ideas At Work!** for your next company, convention, leadership, staff, training, or association event. You'll be glad you did!

Call 1-780-736-0009 to connect with **Bob 'Idea Man' Hooey today!**

Thanks for reading 'Creative Conflict"
Idea-rich leadership strategies for team success

Each time I prepare to step on the stage; each time I sit down to write, or in this case to re-write, I am challenged to ensure I deliver something that will be of **use-it-now value** to my reader.

I ask myself, "If I was reading this, what would I be looking for?"

As well as, "Why is this relevant to me, today?"

These two questions help to keep me focused and help me to remain clear on my objectives. They help to remind me to dig into my experiences, stories, examples, and research to provide solid information that will be of benefit and help my readers, when they apply it, succeed. That can be an exciting challenge!

I trust I have done that for you in this updated primer. **'Creative Conflict' is** my attempt to capture some of the lessons learned *first-hand* serving on various teams and in leadership roles and to share them with you. We need more leaders, now, more than ever. The world is crying out for more compassionate and courageous leaders. I hope you will step up and step into your role as a more effective and influential leader.

Bob in Mumbai, India

I'd love to hear from you and read your success stories. If you would be so kind, please drop me a quick email at: **bob@ideaman.net**

Bob 'Idea Man' Hooey
2011 Spirit of CAPS recipient
www.ideaman.net
www.BobHooey.training
www.HaveMouthWillTravel.com

www.ingramcontent.com/pod-product-compliance
Lightning Source LLC
Chambersburg PA
CBHW030101230526
45471CB00003B/1200